101 Learning Activities

To S T R E T C H and **STRENGTHEN**
Your Child's Multiple Intelligences

Published by Frontsiders, LLC
PO Box 1478
Summerland, CA 93067

Manufactured in the United States of America
First printing July 2012

Table of Contents

Introduction

Each one of us possesses our own unique combination of strengths, preferences and weaknesses across eight distinct intelligences.

When kids are given opportunities to explore the intelligences that they are passionate about, they have a much better chance of achieving a state of flow or practice getting into the "zone"...particularly if those intelligences aren't as readily acknowledged or practiced during the traditional school day.

Further, by "stretching" your kids' least preferred multiple intelligences through play or by combining their least favorite intelligences with the ones they favor, you have an opportunity to stretch understanding in all directions and create an appetite for learning in your kids.

Helping your kids discover interests and strengths early also gives them the best chance of becoming an Outlier (as defined by Malcolm Gladwell), since developing true expertise requires 10,000 hours of focused effort.

No small feat for kids who already spend 1,000 hours each year in the classroom and up to 360 additional hours on homework!

If they're going to spend additional time learning, it should be related to subjects that delight them.

While we've included 101 sample learning activities in this guide, we strongly encourage you to use the exercises as jumping off points or idea starters.

Make them your own! Tailor them to the interests and ages of your family members.

If your child's interests seem to blossom in an intelligence that you're not as excited about, see if you can find local mentors who have turned that particular passion into a career.

Most of all, remember that learning is meant to be *fun*...so have fun with these activities with your family. If your kids don't like an activity, change it up or move on.

Enjoy!

Yay, Learning!

While there are a significant number of people on both sides of the fence as it relates to Brain Gym's trademarked series of movements and whether or not they work, there IS a significant amount of scientific evidence that movement—particularly cross-lateral movement—can help kids anchor thought and prepare for school or homework practice.

Before school starts, why not make up a two-minute "learning cheer" that you and your kids can do together both before the beginning of the school day and before they sit down for homework practice. It helps create a routine (much like a bedtime routine helps prepare kids for impending bedtime), gets blood flowing to the brain. If your child's thought processes ARE, in fact, anchored by the movement, all the better.

Try to incorporate both stretches and calisthenics in your learning cheer. (Especially ones that cross the body's midline!) Or get fancy with some traditional cheerleading jumps.

Sew Cool

While many parents think of sewing as "antiquated" and/or "just for girls," there are plenty of benefits that both your sons and daughters can derive from learning to sew in the kinesthetic intelligence, visual/spatial intelligence, logical/mathematical and naturistic intelligence realms.

Kinesthetically speaking :: From cutting the fabric, to threading the needle, to knotting the thread, to the stitching itself—sewing improves and strengthens fine motor control and hand-eye coordination.

Visually/Spatially speaking :: Your child will be learning to take flat fabric and put together pieces in a way that create a 3-dimensional object...whether it's clothes, a beanbag chair, a Halloween costume, a football, window treatments, a doll, or a hand-made gift for a loved one.

Naturistically speaking :: One of the less-talked-about ways to be green is to mend outfits and shoes with ripped seams or holes worn through in either unseen or unique ways. Or repurpose former clothing, sheets, or window treatments into something completely new and different like tents, bean bags, footballs, quilts, doll clothes, etc.

From a mathematical perspective :: Being able to take a pattern and resize it to make it "custom-fit" takes adding, subtracting and percentage work.

Parking Lot Parade

Getting bikes all gussied up, then parading around on two (or three) wheels with friends is one way to get both fine and gross motor skills moving during summer. And while parents are growing increasingly wary of letting kids play on the street (for good reason), there's one place to hold a neighborhood bike parade that:

- is large enough for all the community's kids to participate,
- EVERYONE can easily find, and
- that isn't seeing much traffic this time of year...

Your Local Elementary or Middle School's Parking Lot!

Half the fun is decorating the bikes, so be sure to give your invitees some potential "bling" hints for the participating bikes. (Better yet, include a theme!!)

- MarthaStewart.com has some great bike bling patterns. Just tape the pattern to some festive wrapping paper and cut along the outside or use white cardstock and have your kids embellish with paints, markers, ribbons, sequins, etc.
- Use crepe paper for wheel spoke weaves.
- Add curling ribbon or balloons to the handle bars.
- Carry favorite stuffed animals in bike baskets.
- Got a musical kid? Put together a soundtrack on a CD, then open all of your car windows and play it for the participants and onlookers, or encourage guests to bring along noisemakers or small instruments.
- Last but not least, don't forget your hats or other head gear from the dress-up box!

Yoga for Young'Uns

Yoga is one kinesthetic activity that kids can enjoy no matter which multiple intelligence lens they prefer to look at the world. Just select an appealing entry point below.

Visual-Spatial kids: Without worrying about movement flow at first, challenge your picture smart learner not only to mirror each pose you do, but to see how their constellation of body parts creates the pose name's shape like tree, cobra, or warrior.

Linguistic kids: Make up a story to tell through each pose in your yoga practice—the cobra reared its head, which made the dog bristle and bow down; then the warrior took aim at the cobra under the light of the half moon.

Musical kids: Key into the rhythm/fluidity of movements through poses that match in/out breaths.

Logical/Mathematical kids: work on yogic breathwork. Not just in/out matching based on counts, but in for 2 beats through one nostril, hold for beats x 2, out 2 beats through other nostril. Reverse.

Intrapersonal/Interpersonal kids: key into the historical, religious and meditative ties to intrapersonal development and growth.

Naturistic kids: key into the natural qualities of each pose —tree pose is rooted in the earth with branches reaching toward the sky.

Dancing Outside the Box

When many of us picture ourselves dancing, we think of movements inside a small box (prom-style)—or moving side-to-side with small arm movements close to our bodies. And even for kids who've taken dance classes, many think of dance as repeating movements the teacher asks them to perform.

However, when we think of the dances that truly evoke emotion in the audience (So-You-Think-You-Can-Dance-style), they speak through movement. By introducing your children to the overarching vocabulary of dance in a safe space at home, you'll be giving them a new language to express emotion and identity.

Dance "speaks" through:

- SPACE. Does what you're feeling make you want to make BIG movements or small movements? What levels or direction do you want to move? (backward? sideways? in a zig-zag? up and down?)
- TIME. How fast do you want to move? Do you want to move with the beat or hold some positions longer and make other movements more quickly?
- ENERGY. Do you feel heavy or light during your dance? Do you want to move smoothly or use rougher movements?
- BODY. Are you moving just parts of your body or the whole thing? Are you moving one side of your body at a time or are both sides mirror images of each other?
- MOVEMENT. Are you walking? Jumping? Skipping? Rolling? Bending? Twisting? Melting? Spinning?

Font Formation

Did you know that being body smart doesn't just mean having great gross motor skills, but having fierce fine motor skills, as well?

Today, strengthen your fingers by creating your own stylized fonts! Using a black pen, create upper- and lower-case versions of the alphabet and import a font that's 100% yours into a font generator like yourfonts.com.

Want to get fancy? Get yourself some calligraphy pens.

Bonus: you can use the fonts in your favorite Microsoft Office, Adobe or OpenOffice documents.

Go for the Juggler

Besides being fun, juggling is a great way to flex your body smarts. It's well known that juggling improves your hand-eye coordination, which will improve your game in pretty much every other sport, and also helps kids become more ambidextrous.

What most people don't realize, however, is that juggling can help certain areas of your brain grow! In fact, a 2004 neuroscience study divided 24 non-jugglers into two groups and assigned one group to practice juggling for three months. The scientists performed MRI brain scans on the volunteers before and after they learned to juggle. The dozen folks who did not learn to juggle showed NO difference in their brain scans over the three-month period. The group that DID learn to juggle showed an increase in both volume and density in gray matter in two areas of the brain.

Now that's flexing your body smarts.

Want to take a crack at it? Googling "how to juggle" returns 5.8 million different results, but we think this YouTube video is entertaining and informative.

http://www.youtube.com/watch?v=ln5cMKfD8SA

Kine-Simon

Do you remember the old My Simon game that was a family favorite back when we were kids? Update that concept with Kine-Simon for some active family fun that tests your memory muscles as well as your physical ones.

To play...
1. Pick a game leader.
2. Have the leader decide on four movements that everyone playing can perform like clap, jump, spin, squat.
3. Leader makes one movement and players repeat the move.
4. Then, leader adds a second movement and players repeat both movements.
5. Play continues at an increasingly rapid and lengthy pace.
6. If a player gets the sequence wrong, they are OUT.
7. Last player remaining gets to be leader the next time.

Make the game more challenging based on your family's physical abilities and rhythmic talents with more challenging movements; stretched out holds such as touch your toes for 3 seconds, followed by 3 second tree pose, followed by 3 second half moon pose; or by combining sound and movement like vibrating your lips while rolling your arms.

Forgoing Fear of Failure

In an era of teaching to the test in school and avoiding mistakes at all costs, one of the most important things we need to teach our children these days is that failure in and of itself is not a negative thing. It's how we react to failure—or overcome fear of failure—that really counts.

Talk to your children about some famous "failures" or quotes from successful historical figures that they can relate to. For instance:

- Beethoven's music teacher once said, "As a composer, he is hopeless."
- Thomas Edison's reaction after 8,000 unsuccessful trials on a nickel-iron storage battery was, "Well, at least we know 8,000 things that won't work."
- Michael Jordan was cut from his high school basketball team due to "lack of skill."
- A newspaper editor once told Walt Disney that he had no good ideas for film production.

Then, decide on one body smart skill—like riding a bike, doing a cartwheel, hitting a baseball at the batting cages, catching a football, or playing a song on the piano—that each family member has not yet mastered and work together as a family to help everyone master those skills. In this way, family members learn to give advice in a way that others can relate to, that also doesn't shame or frustrate the learner. And the child receiving the advice will get practice graciously accepting constructive criticism from others.

Out of the Box Gaming

Much of the appeal of video games for kids lies in flexing their logic/strategy muscles and developing spatial aptitude via the game's fast action and leveled challenges—not to mention getting the opportunity to be a "hero"—all of which can be translated into active summer fun with a little creativity.

Grab a few squirt guns from the dollar store and make an obstacle course in your backyard or a local park that your child has to navigate along a set path without getting wet.

Start with just a few obstacles with no time limit. Increase the challenge by adding more obstacles or putting a time limit on goal achievement. Let your child alternate roles between "hero" and "bad guy," since both sides will require different strategies. One of the keys to remember within video game setups is that, in most cases, there's one "hero" and multiple "bad guys". So, if possible, ask friends or other family members to join the fun.

Extra Credit: Make the game even more interesting by adding treasures to collect along the way—hide rewards of random collected objects that your child enjoys like a movie rental, reprieve from one chore for a day, a favorite pack of gum, extra bedtime story, etc.

Melodramatic Mime

Have your child act out a favorite story or book in melodramatic mime, playing all the characters. Encourage over-exaggerated movements from her!

Extra Credit: Have your child mime one of your favorite stories without you reading it. See if you can figure out from the melodrama which story she's acting out.

Take Up Tai Chi

Tai chi has recently been found to increase brain size and benefit cognition in a randomized, controlled trial of Chinese elderly. While the findings were based on a study of 60-70 year-olds, we think tai chi has similar benefits for kids.

Cari Shurman, Founder and Creator of Tai Chi Moves for Kids, agrees. "Tai Chi works on the inside of the body and helps give order to feelings of confusion and turmoil. We begin to understand our needs and emotions and to anticipate a feeling that is building in us. It becomes easier to find self-control. Pretending to be an animal moving peacefully in nature takes us away from the noisy, hectic pace of daily life."

Dip your toe in the water with this sample introductory lesson for kids on YouTube:
http://www.youtube.com/watch?v=5cANSD9G6Wc&t=3m8s

To get Cari Shurman's program, Tai Chi Moves for Kids, which includes 12 cards with pictures and explanations of the movements in addition to a DVD and audio CD for regular practice, go here:
http://www.taichiforkids.com/buy

Have a Field Day

Take a cue from the hit show Minute to Win It and have each of your family members come up with 3-4 games in which you can compete against each other.

You can choose any of the Minute to Win It games; any "normal" track and field event that you can safely play in your backyard or at a park; or get creative and come up with a timed body smart activity of your own!

Purchase the necessary supplies for your Field Day. Then, over Saturday or Sunday night dinner, reveal the events in your field day and give everyone a week to practice the events. Order gold, silver and bronze medals for each event or make your own out of ribbon and construction paper.

NEXT WEEKEND
- Grab a digital timer or smartphone to time the events.
- Each family member needs to attempt to complete each event.
- Have an awards ceremony for the winners of each event.

Extra Credit: Capture it all on camera, then make a scrapbook of the field day for posterity.

Generate More Body Smart Fun

Need more body smart inspiration? Fun is literally just three clicks away with the Fun Generator!

http://www.nhs.uk/Change4Life/Pages/fun-generator.aspx

(Also available on iPad, iPhone or Android devices here: http://www.nhs.uk/Change4Life/Pages/fun-generator-mobile.aspx)

1. Click whether you want to play indoors or outdoors,
2. select the number of people joining in the fun, then
3. click GO.

Audible Feast

As we all know, variety is the spice of life…but many of us get stuck in a rut when it comes to the musical genres we listen to.

When you think about it, though, music is much like food in the sense that just because you don't like salmon cooked a certain way at one restaurant doesn't mean you won't devour it when it's cooked differently by another chef.

Commit to expanding your family's musical "taste buds" by spending at least ONE hour a week experiencing an out of the ordinary musical genre as a family. You don't need to love it, but try to appreciate the layers and complexity of each "taste" you get just as you (the parents, of course) would if you went wine tasting.

Luckily, this exercise is piece of cake in the age of cable, satellite TV and the Internet. Go to one of the music channels that you wouldn't normally select on your preferred device, put on the timer for an hour, then PUT DOWN THE MOUSE or remote.

Unless there's a lot of profanity in the lyrics, don't change the station or turn off the channel.

What instruments do you hear in the music? Are they different or similar to the ones used in the music you nomally listen to? How do the rhythms differ? What do you think of the lyrics? Is the music melodic or dissonant? Is there more of a variation in dynamics like transitions from loud to soft or vice-versa?

Personal Soundtracks

I don't know about you, but my favorite
cassettes and CDs as a kid were movie
soundtracks. They were the ones that best
"put me in the mood" for whatever it was I needed to get
accomplished...or however I wanted to feel.

Rather than having Pandora or Slacker pick out your kids' tunes
this week, have them make up their own playlists for:
- waking up
- cleaning up
- playing
- studying
- winding down
- going to bed
- etc.

Then, use their preferred music player to play their personal
soundtrack to get in the mood for whatever it is you need them
to do.

Extra Credit: See if just turning their personal soundtrack on
gets your kids doing what you need them to do!

Signature Sound

If you ever read a musician's biography or an interview with a modern-day maestro, you'll often find at least one passage about the other artists, composers or time periods that influenced the individual musically. This musical "geneaology" helps us trace the roots of the musician's signature sound.

In most classical and some contemporary music pieces, you'll find what are called variations on a theme. The music will sound similar, but there will be something different about it— often, more notes will be added to the melody (called melodic ornamentation) or the rhythms, harmonies or keys will change. When you read about a musician's musical influences, you can often listen to their music with fresh ears and hear variations on themes from the artists that influenced them.

Today, try to reveal your own signature sound.

What musical pieces are your favorites? What makes you like them so much? Do they have similar chord progressions? Rhythms? Do they use similar instruments? Are the singers male or female? Solo or group performers? Do the songs sound happy, sad, or spooky...or do they evoke a different emotion? Do you "tune into" certain types of lyrics?

Extra Credit: Is your signature sound similar to or different from your friends' and family members'? What makes it similar or different?

Skillful Singing

For most adults, recalling the alphabet goes hand-in-hand with singing the tune, as do many of the concepts we learned in school. For musical kids, this effect is even more pronounced.

Chat with your child about some of the language or math concepts she finds challenging. Then, have her come up with tunes to remember the rules or concepts ("what's a pronoun?", "I before E except after C", "a silent E turns other vowels long", etc.).

Need inspiration? Flocabulary.com has hundreds of original songs that are aligned with K-12 concepts in all of the major subject areas.

Forces of Nature

Play some nature-based music like George Winston's seasons-based piano solos from the early 1980s. Have your child pretend to be either the forces of nature (wind, storm, rain) or the animals that they think would be in the scene, based on the title and musical score.

How do your child's movements differ from piece to piece? What does he hear in the music that makes him spin vs. run vs. tiptoe vs. stomp?

Extra Credit: Now turn the music *off*. Go outside for inspiration and shout out different forces of nature or animals for your child to act out.

The Music of Poetry

Pick up a copy of *The Music Lover's Poetry Anthology* (Houghton, Draper & McClatchy, 2007) at a library or bookstore.

Choose a few of the poems you think your child would enjoy, then download some of the musical pieces by the composers who were the poets' muses.

Talk about some of your child's favorite composers or artists. Do some biographical research to find out more about their lives.

Then have your child create an original poem that is rhythmically similar to the tune (or part of the tune) of one of the composer's pieces that talks about his or her life.

Extra Credit: Enjoy *Hip Hop Speaks to Children with CD: A Celebration of Poetry with a Beat* (Giovanni, de Dios, Ward & Balouch, 2008) with your child.

The International Language

Play a song with lyrics in a language that your child doesn't know in a style that appeals to him.

What does it sound like the singer might be talking about?
What is it about the music that makes him think so?
The rhythm?
Order of notes (chord progression)?
The way the lyrics are sung?

Find a translation of the words online and see how closely the prediction matched the reality.

Extra Credit: Take one of your child's favorite poems or stories and set it to music selected by your child as a good "fit" with rewritten lyrics.

'Tis the Season

Play a piece of classical music that is
supposed to take place during a certain
season.

Can your child guess what season the
composer wanted you to see in your mind's eye?

What about the music helps you see that season?
Instruments?
Articulations? (staccato, sustained, vibrato) Melody?
Harmonies?
Dynamics? (forte, piano)
Tempo?

Extra Credit: Which of the aspects of music (generally
speaking) would your child use to "describe" different zoo
animals?

Hearing in Color

Using a pitch pipe, have your child picture different colors as you play each note on the scale (red for C, orange for D, yellow for E, green for F, aqua for G, blue for A, purple for B).

After repeating several times, play a random note and ask what color s/he saw in their mind's eye.

Did they hit the mark? Were they close?

Extra Credit: Once your child starts connecting color with tone this way, try it with different octaves...then with chords.

Rhythm Nation

Talk about the different types of notes (whole, half, quarter, eighth, sixteenth) as well as the time signature or meter.

Talk about how, just like in math, each measure has to make up the number of beats in the time signature.

Using a metronome, see if your child can pat out the melody that's written on the page.

Extra Credit: Have your child try to transcribe the rhythm of a piece of music onto sheet music, using a metronome. (Don't worry about the notes.) Look at the actual sheet music. How close did he come?

Family Theme Song

Decide on a piece of music that will be your family theme song.

What about it made your children choose that song?

The lyrics?
The tempo?
The melody?
How about theme songs for each individual family member?

Extra Credit: Have your kids add verses to your family theme song for each family member—Weird Al Yankovic style.

Audible Feast

As we all know, variety is the spice of life...but many of us get stuck in a rut when it comes to the musical genres we listen to.

When you think about it, though, music is much like food in the sense that just because you don't like salmon cooked a certain way at one restaurant doesn't mean you won't devour it when it's cooked differently by another chef.

Commit to expanding your family's musical "taste buds" by spending at least ONE hour a week experiencing an out of the ordinary musical genre as a family. You don't need to love it, but try to appreciate the layers and complexity of each "taste" you get just as you (the parents, of course) would if you went wine tasting.

Luckily, this exercise is piece of cake in the age of cable, satellite TV and the Internet. Go to one of the music channels that you wouldn't normally select on your preferred device, put on the timer for an hour, then PUT DOWN THE MOUSE or remote.

Unless there's a lot of profanity in the lyrics, don't change the station or turn off the channel.

What instruments do you hear in the music? Are they different or similar to the ones used in the music you nomally listen to? How do the rhythms differ? What do you think of the lyrics? Is the music melodic or dissonant? Is there more of a variation in dynamics like transitions from loud to soft or vice-versa?

The Zen Zone

No one is disputing the many benefits of meditation, which has been proven in an astounding number of studies to relieve stress or anxiety and replace tension with inner peace.

Too bad meditation (sitting still and breathing with a clear mind) is not as easy as it may sound! Mental to-do lists are hard to silence and, for kids, sitting still for the recommended minute per year of age per day may seem like an eternity...particularly when they're used to the fast, scattered pace of television or computer games.

For many people, music helps them get their meditation on. Over the course of the next week, focus on what sounds help you get "in the zone"...and stay there!

Some people like chanting, others prefer drumming, still others prefer instrumentals or nature sounds like running streams, waves crashing on the shore, or birds singing in the forest. Still others think there's magic in megahertz (Hz).

Experiment and see what works best for you!

Striped Celery

Adapted from *Science Experiments You Can Eat: Revised Edition* (Cobb, 1984)

We often focus on plant leaves converting sun into energy for plants... and on the roots "drinking" the water that the plant needs. Without the xylem in the stems, however, the water would never make it from the roots to the leaves! The xylem is like a pipeline filled made up of hollow cells.

To see this botanical boulevard at work, you'll need:
- four leafy stalks of celery,
- red food coloring,
- a small, clear plastic bag,
- a timer, and
- two see-through glasses.

Put 1 teaspoon of red food coloring in each of your water glasses and fill them halfway up. Next, cut the ends of two of the celery stalks horizontally so that you can see the xylem pipelines. Then, cut the leaves off one of the stalks. Now, place the non-leafy celery stalk and a leafy celery stalk in ONE glass and turn on your timer. How long does it take each stalk to carry the food coloring to the top?

Now, you're ready for part 2! In this part, cut the non-leafy ends off of the two remaining leafy celery stalks and place them in a glass with colored water in a sunny location. Now, put a small, clear plastic bag over one of the stalks. Start your timer. Which stalk carried the water fastest? Slowest? Why do you believe this is? *(Hint: It has to do with evaporation!)*

Explore New Places

While you probably know the parks close by your house very well, we're betting there are a ton you haven't seen or experienced yet! ExploreYourParks.com has highlighted the many unique places to explore nature within our state parks... and even has activity guides, hiking tips, park passes, camping programs and more in select regions. The site also has some terrific general getting started tips/guides.

Use the park locator to highlight a few places in your area that you want to explore this summer and make plans to visit them with friends or family.

Butterflies & Blooms

Set a goal to help restore butterfly migration routes in your town by planting a butterfly garden with native plants or seeds.

Research the best options to provide nectar, roosting, or food for caterpillars that migrate through your area. If it's in a place that's visible to neighbors, have your child post a sign letting your neighbors know what it is and what's been planted to help make a difference for your floating friends.

Maybe your child will inspire others in your area to do the same!

Environmental Experiments

Set up a summer-long experiment to see how small changes in environment affect plants. Begin by planting identical plant seeds or young plants in five different containers and decide on different watering schedules or quantities for each plant. (You can use cut-off milk cartons or plastic bottles for your pots.)

Once a week, measure the growth of each plant. In which conditions did the plants grow best? How about worst? Want to try more? Repeat the experiment with the optimal water level in varying light levels: shade, partial sun, full sun, indoors.

Extra Credit: Grow a plant that's native to your area in one pot next to a similarly sized plant that's native to a more humid or warmer environment, and/or another that's native to a dryer or colder environment, all of which prefer the same light levels. Don't water any of the plants, and see the differences in how each plant struggles or flourishes.

Sing Like a Bird

Pop Quiz: How many cereal brands can your child name? How about fast food restaurants? Now ask him/her to name all the birds s/he can remember. There are probably just as many bird species in your neighborhood as fast-food brands (if not more!), yet most 9 year-old kids can only name two types of birds.

Help your child get in touch with his feathered friends by learning about the different bird calls/voices of your area's native species. Then, go outside and see if he can distinguish each bird's "voice". Does your child hear more of one vs. another? Are there some birds that seem to be more talkative in the morning vs. midday vs. the evening?

Extra Credit: See if your child can mimic local bird calls. Can he strike up a "conversation" that brings the birds closer?

Backyard Bug Banquet

Use your child's gifts for observation and analysis and use your backyard or nearby park as a math and science lab.

One way Deborah Churchman of American Forests suggests is to mix overripe fruit and honey in a blender, then go outside at sunset and spread the mixture on a few trees.

Go back with a flashlight with your child when it's dark and see what creatures are feasting on your backyard banquet.

Try it with a different combination of fruit and sweetener (agave nectar, sugar, molasses) on a different night.

Which one attracted more bugs? Were certain insects drawn to one more than the other?

Letter Perfect Park Poems

Adapted with permission from Chicago Park District's "Once Upon a Day Camp" Guide

Go to a park or into another natural setting (beach, woods, etc.) with your child. Choose something you see to compose a letter perfect poem (a poem in which each line starts with the same letter) together. Then, have her choose a different subject in the environment (wave, rock, vine) and try it on her own. If she gets stuck, brainstorm other words that start with the same letter together.

Extra Credit: Read selections from a poetry anthology like *Color Me a Rhyme: Nature Poems for Young People* (Yolen, 2003) with your child.

Native Nature

Encourage your child's "blossoming" love of nature by introducing the art of xeriscaping. Have her help you identify new plants that you can use to beautify your outdoor surroundings...that can thrive without additional irrigation.

As you try out a few of the native plant suggestions in your yard, pots or planter boxes, talk about why it's so important to conserve water.

Extra Credit: Take it to the streets! Have your child offer suggestions to local influencers of ways to incorporate xeriscaping principles into local school yards, parks, business parks, etc.

For the Birds

Help encourage your child to learn more about your neighborhood's feathered friends by putting out different kinds of food (bird seed, bread crumbs, cracker pieces, cereal, jelly) or use food coloring and try different colored sugar water in a bowl.

Track which colors and foods attract the most birds.

If this is an activity that your child enjoys, keep it going for several months. Do your visitors differ during different times of year?

Extra Credit: Take pictures of your bird buffet patrons with a cell phone camera and see which types of food or colors each individual bird type prefers. Learn the characteristics, names, and categorizations of the birds.

Secret Hideout

Go to a nearby "wild" space with a few of your child's friends and help the kids create a "secret hideout" solely from the trees, rocks, branches, etc.

Show the kids how they can use the hideout for more than just club meetings: by using the flora and fauna from the area to disguise themselves, they create a "blind" from which they can see the way animals and birds act and interact when they don't think any humans are watching.

Extra Credit: Grab a pair of binoculars and a camera phone and get closer to the action as a wildlife photographer. (Just put the lens of the camera phone over one of the "eyes" of the binoculars.)

Sensory Sensitivities

Visit different outdoor environments—
the playground, a field, the woods,
school, your backyard, a community
garden, the zoo, the beach. Or visit the same one at different
times of day with your child and tune into your senses.

What does she see, feel, smell, hear...even taste? How are they
different? Which sense is strongest in which environments...or
at which times of day?

Extra Credit: Go into the same environment(s) the day
that thunderstorms are forecast or when it's cloudy. What
differences does your child notice via her senses in the different
types of weather? Could she use this knowledge to predict

weather in the future?

Native Notebook

One of the primary aspects of nature smarts is the ability to classify and categorize our native "habitats".

Today, find a list of the native plants, birds and trees in your neck of the woods. Then, print them out and staple them into a Native Notebook. (You can use the spiral-bound, perfect-bound, or looseleaf variety.)

When you happen upon a new species, take a picture with your camera phone, then note the location in your notebook. Print the picture out on your printer and paste it next to the location in your notebook, then cross the species off your list.

See how long it takes you to find all of the plants, trees and animals on your list!

Extra Credit: Put a local map on your wall and buy some pushpins. When you find a new species, pinpoint the location of your discovery with a pushpin!

Nature Smart Activity

Have you ever noticed that it smells different when it rains? Or that you can tell it's going to be a hot day by the AM aroma?

When you wake up to different weather, try to tie the weather pattern to how things smell. (Like grown ups do with wine.)

Does impending rain make any nearby flowers more fragrant?

Does a hotter day make the outside smell like mushrooms?

Note these differences and see how early you can tell what weather you'll experience next.

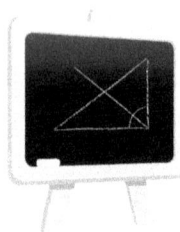

Score Well in Math

Inspired by Super Bowl Sub Game from *Teaching Math to People with Down Syndrome and Other Hands-On Learners* (Horstmeier, 2004)

Here's a fun way to remember the rules of your favorite sport and practice math skills at the same time.

PREPARATION
1. Have your child pick a sport, then print out the game board (AKA field) from a bevy of choices on SportsDiagrams.com.
2. Look up the official rules of the game and write them on index cards.
3. Separate the good ones and bad ones into two different piles. For instance, "Kicked field goal! Score 3 points" in the "good" pile and "Offsides – go back 10 yards" in the bad pile.
4. Put the math skill you are practicing on a set of index cards. fractions, division, or addition, for example.

PLAY
1. Set a time limit for the game.
2. Pick a card from the math skill pile.
3. Once the player has the answer, the other player must check his/her work against a calculator.
4. If correct, the player takes an instruction card from the GOOD pile and does as instructed.
5. If incorrect, the player takes an instruction card from the BAD pile and does as instructed.
6. Play continues until time runs out and the player with the highest score wins.

Nutrition Math

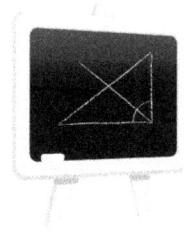

One of the most important things we can teach our kids during our current obesity epidemic is the basics of eating right. And *many* of those basics are grounded in math...from portion control to how much of what foods to eat.

Plated Portion Police :: Using the USDA's MyPlate recommendation, make your kids the "plate police" at dinner. Does everyone in the family have the right proportions of food on their plate? How much more of each food needs to be added? Taken away? Talk in fractions.

Grocery Graph :: Talk about eating a variety of proteins and grains and a rainbow of fruits and vegetables, then make a weekly chart or graph of food types to include.
Bring it along to the grocery store and empower your kids to help you select what will be served at meals during the week, then have them be responsible for making tally marks (or filling in graph squares) to ensure you're spicing up the family's lifestyle with enough variety.
Sample Graph: kidzmet.com/files/grocery-graph2.pdf

Chew On This Checklist :: Kaboose.com has some handy checklists that you can use as jumping off points for conversations. For example, "You can have one grain serving in your lunchbox today. You've put 7 crackers in so far. How many do you need to take away?" or "You've got half a banana on your plate for breakfast this morning. How much more fruit can you eat today?"

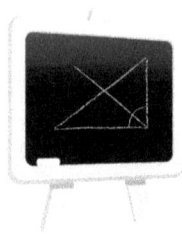

Math Frisbee Golf

Frisbee (or disc) golf is a fun way for the whole family to get some low-intensity activity on pleasant sunny days. And while a "normal" game of disc golf sharpens hand/eye coordination and visual/spatial skills, it's easy to sprinkle in some math practice with a few flash cards in the back pocket (separate decks for each kid).

Preparation
- Decide on the math skill that each family member is going to work on (including the grownups!) and make up 25 flash cards with both equations and answers. Then head to an open space with at least one frisbee.
- Together, plot out a course/sequence of six object "holes" at which the Frisbee will be aimed. The objects can be anything from trees to jackets to cones...as long as the "hole" doesn't move during play.

Play
Once the course is decided, players must answer a flash card correctly to take a turn attempting to hit the targets with the Frisbee. If answered incorrectly, the player doesn't get to throw the frisbee, but the turn is still counted on the score card.

Scoring
- Each turn (whether the frisbee is thrown or not) counts as a tally mark for each player.
- The player who completes the course in the fewest number of throws wins.

Outdoor Board Game

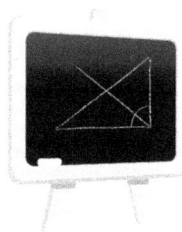

Thumb ball "die" inspired by Mike & Chelsea Ashcraft of Children's Choice

Go outside with a piece of chalk and draw an outdoor gameboard like what you see on Candy Land. (A long series of squares with a "start" and an "end".)

Make the game board as long as possible, with a minimum of at least 50 squares.

Now, in random squares, write an action like "cackle like a witch," "skip forward 5 squares," "take two long steps backward," or "twirl backward 10 squares."

Finally, blow up a multi-colored beach ball and use a sharpie to draw an "equator" on the ball, then number each section from 1 to 12.

Now you're ready to play!

Toss the ball to the first player. Add together whatever numbers your thumbs land on. Then, move forward that many spaces. Take whatever action the square says to take, then toss the ball to the next player.

Whoever crosses the finish line first wins!

Haiku and Tanka

Pick up a child-friendly Haiku collection like *If Not for the Cat* (Jack Prelutsky, 2004) or *Cricket Never Does* (Myra Cohn Livingston, 1997) to introduce your child to the art and science of Haiku and Tanka.

Talk about the structure of Haiku (5 syllables in the first line, 7 syllables in the second line, 5 syllables in the third line) and Tanka (a Haiku plus two additional 7 syllable lines) and how their beauty is in the preciseness of their respective forms...and how you need to choose your words wisely to make it work.

Have your child try writing their own haikus and tankas about favorite activities, places or people.

Extra Credit: If he took to the initial activity, have him try a cinquain next (2 syllables in line 1, 4 syllables in line 2, 6 syllables in line 3, 8 syllables in line 4, 2 syllables in line 5).

Race to the Finish

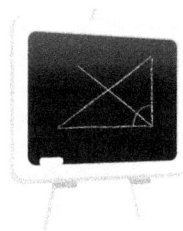

Grab a piece of graph paper, 2 colored pencils, 1 marker, 2 numbered dice (either traditional or 12 sided), a calculator and an optional timer.

Draw a line "path" on the graph paper. The path can't cross anywhere on the paper, must be separated by at least 2 squares around all bends, start and end must be indicated.

Based on your child's ability level, decide whether you'll be practicing number recognition (just one die), addition (both dice) or multiplication (both dice). If you've got an extra die, you can kick things up a notch with a third number.

HOW TO PLAY:
Step 1: Roll the dice and figure out the solution in your head (either what number was rolled, the multiplied result, or the added result).
Step 2: Have the other player confirm the solution on the calculator. (You can make it harder by timing it with an egg timer or iPhone timer or even award a certain number of "bonus squares" for figuring out the solution in under 5 or 10 seconds.)
Step 3: Have the player who solved the problem fill in the appropriate number of squares along the LEFT side of the path with their colored pencil.
Step 4: Have the other player repeat on the RIGHT side of the path.

The first player to cross the finish line wins the race!

Numbers in the News

Every day, attention-getting numbers are released in the news. In fact, there's a significant amount of data that shows that headlines with digits are shared more widely on digital media than those without. While some of them are not for kids'-consumption, there are some really cool "did you know" numbers that also make headlines and *are* appropriate.

This summer, challenge your family to a weekly "did you know" dinner and talk about some of the most amazing numbers you've seen in the news during the week.

While the grown-ups and older kids at the table can scan the normal news headlines, you'll probably want to steer younger kids toward these sitess that are content-curated to be appropriate for a young audience.

Science: Science News for Kids
World News: TIME for Kids
Sports: Sports Illustrated for Kids
Nature: National Geographic for Kids
Animals: Kind News (through the Humane Society)

Seeing is Believing
Take your findings a step further and put those numbers in perspective for the kids. For instance, got a "million" number you're talking about? Talk about how there are a million grains of sand in 1 cup and that's how many people you're talking about.

Calculation Compositions

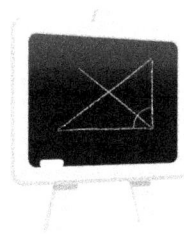

If your child is learning to read music, they are also learning math...sometimes without even realizing it! By pointing out the correlations between math and music, your child will begin to see the parallels between the two realms.

A few examples of how you can illustrate examples for each concept include:

- If your child is in preschool or kindergarten, have her mimic or extend the note patterns or rhythm patterns you start. For instance, you play C C E D C C E D, then s/he plays C C E D or pat/pat/clap/snap.
- If a piece is written in 4/4 time, how many quarter notes are in each measure? If your child is learning 5 or 10 groups, show him how these separations are like measures in a musical piece.
- If your child is learning multiplication, have her multiply by measures. (If there are 8 measures in the piece with 4/4 time, then how many quarter notes are there in the whole piece? How about eighth notes?)
- If she is learning to graph, remind her that written music graphs notes on a ledger in the same way that we graph numbers on an axis.

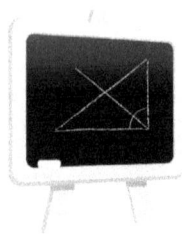

Timing is Everything

Take a look at what was expected of your child in the math and language arts realm during their last year of school and what lies ahead in the next school year.

If you're in one of the 45 states that have adopted the common core, you can see exactly what was and will be expected of them on corestandards.org.

Make a summer action plan: first, how you'll tackle each of the concepts; and second, how much time your child is willing to dedicate to math work each week. Finally, decide on an associated reward for staying true to the time commitment.

When the reward is achieved for meeting the time commitment, see how closely the original time estimate for concept mastery is to the actual timeline, and adjust the time commitment and/ or timeline accordingly.

Bonus! Working with time management skills in this way over the summer can be parlayed into homework/study planning in the fall.

Become a Story Sleuth

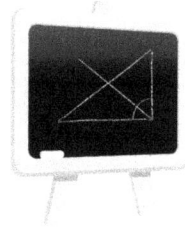

Tie together logic and language with whodunit puzzles!

Playing detective once a day will strengthen both your child's word and number smarts in an enjoyable way.

Amazon has a huge selection of whodunits from which to choose at this link:
http://amzn.to/m4tplv

Extra Credit: Time how quickly puzzles are solved and charting the solution speed over time to add even more math to the mysteries.

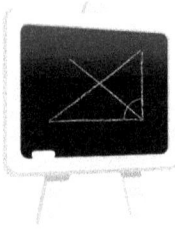

Drive a Hard Bargain

Garage sales give kids a weekly way to practice math skills with a tangible reward at the end. This week, have your child gather their weekly allowance and hit the garage sale circuit. If you want to, practice bargaining before you head out—for instance, if something is marked as $2, offer $1, then go up incrementally until the seller agrees.

Bring along a small notebook to mark the item, how much it was originally priced at the yard sale, and how much your child paid for it. Then, go home and see how much that item would have cost at retail.

If your child is in the older elementary grades, add two columns to the notebook:
1. How much of a discount off the garage sale price he was able to get, and
2. how much of a discount off the RETAIL price he scored.

Tally the totals of
1. all of his purchases' prices,
2. how much he paid in total,
3. how much it would have cost him to buy those items retail.

You've not only snuck in math practice on the weekend, but taught your child the true value of reuse.

Extra Credit: After several weeks of practice, hold a garage sale of your own and make money off of the items around your house, using the pricing strategies you've developed as a result of your "field tests."

Famous Formulas

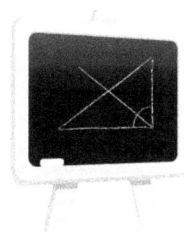

As grown-ups, we use formulas all the time without remembering WHY we use them or HOW they came into being.

Today, talk with your child about how some of the most famous formulas came to be. Here are a few examples to get you started:

Pi
"π (pi), has puzzled mathematicians for nearly four thousand years, generating more interest, consuming more brainpower, and filling more waste baskets with discarded theories than any other single number...you will never find an exact value for π." The Joy of Pi. Blatner, D. (1999) Loads of Pi trivia can be found at http://www.eveandersson.com/pi/trivia/?

Irrational Numbers
Legend has it that less than 2500 years ago, the Pythagoreans mathematicians (credited with the Pythagorean theorem) took a vow of secrecy when they discovered irrational numbers (a number that cannot be expressed as a fraction) so this mathematical idea was kept under wraps for nearly 200 years under penalty of death! Irrational numbers are the basis for the Fibonacci sequence—also referred to as the square root spiral.

E = mc2
Einstein arrived at his famous formula by taking a wild guess! Once he guessed at the formula, he backed into the mathematical and scientific reasoning...he didn't get there from the ground up.

But there is plenty of mathematical history yet to be written. In fact, in May 2012 a 16-year-old German student cracked a 350 year-old mathematical riddle first posed by Isaac Newton.

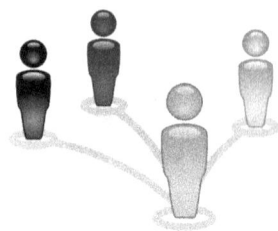

Cultural Care Package

I don't know how it is in your house, but at our house, getting something in the snail mail box is always a thrill for my kids.

I must admit, I was the same way when I was young. I even had a Japanese pen pal and we would compare notes about life in the U.S. versus life in Japan.

I came across Little Passports the other day and thought it was a great way to get kids excited about other cultures. From geography to history and culture to language. These pen pals send an educational care package once a month that's been designed for elementary aged kids.

Filled with souvenirs, activity sheets, arts and crafts projects, stickers, postcards, photos from the country, map markers, etc., the package provides access to even more online games and activities.

The Art of Introductions

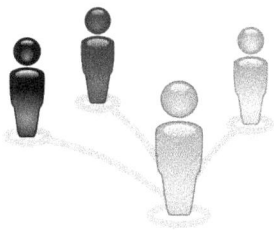

One of the best ways to flex your people smarts is to practice introducing people who don't know each other yet. Sounds easy, but even some grown-ups struggle with the art of introductions! As with all other skills, it takes practice.

Do you know any kids who don't know each other that you think would get along well? Today, your mission is to invite two friends over for a playdate at your house or at the park and help them get to know each other.

As the host, it's your job to get your friends talking. You can start the conversation by saying BOTH people's names and talking about something they both enjoy, something interesting that happened to one of them recently, or something that one of them is proud of or recently accomplished. For instance:

- "Amy, this is my friend Jill. You and Jill both like to play soccer!"
- "Justin, this is my friend Bob. Bob went to Yosemite last year and saw a grizzly bear! Pretty neat, huh?"
- "Blossom, this is my friend Rose. I met Rose at tai kwon do last year. She just earned her brown belt!"

Remember that some kids are shy, so you may need to offer up a few ideas of things your friends have in common or interesting "fun facts" about both of them before the conversation really starts rolling on its own.

Conversation Placemats

One of the best places for kids to practice the art of conversation is at the dinner table. But, too often, these conversations can go as stale as a week-old piece of bread. Who wants to have the same old conversations over and over again?

Starting tonight, cook up more interesting conversational topics with conversation placemats. You can make your own or print out several of the ones on this link, then laminate the placemats.

http://www.kidzmet.com/files/dinner-dish.pdf

Hand the placemats out before dinner each evening and have each family member write their conversation topics with dry-erase markers and then place the mats at the table. You can even go for theme nights—funniest "did you know" topics, neighborhood news topics, pet stories, wish lists, etc.

You might find family members are experts in areas you never expected!

Now You're Cooking!

Stretch both your child's verbal and math skills by trying "worldly" recipes together. Whether you use the Internet or your library card, immerse your family in a new culture each week over dinner.

Read about local customs and history and talk about the new information you've discovered each night during the week at dinner.

Over the course of the week, read regional recipes and decide on the ones that sound most appealing for a family dinner.

Make a shopping list together for the ingredients (including quantities) you'll need for the recipes you've selected.

Then, figure out timing—what time do you need to get started to finish dinner on time? How much do you need of each ingredient? Figure out quantities based on different measuring cups and spoons: if you need four cups of an ingredient, how many 1/3 cup measures do you need in the mixing bowl? If you need three tablespoons of an ingredient, how many teaspoons would this be?)

When eating your cultural feast, get fancy and use a variety of vocabulary words to describe each dish, or learn key words and phrases from its country of origin and use them during the meal.

After Happily Ever After

Choose a favorite story to act out as a family...but don't start at the beginning—start at the END!

Have each family member choose a different character to play and act out what happens next in the character's lives.

Extra Credit: Every few minutes, say "SWITCH" and have everyone switch characters, then continue the plot, playing different roles. Enjoy how the story twists and turns as the dynamics between the characters change.

Be Playful

Have your child become a playwright. Take his natural gift for language and storytelling and apply it to playwriting.

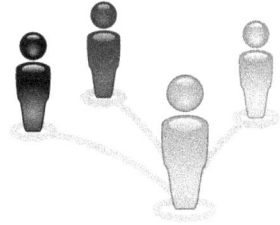

Creating dialogue, imagining character motivations and developing story arcs will help your child strengthen interpersonal smarts in a way that's comfortable for both extroverts and introverts.

Extra Credit: Facilitate a small neighborhood production and invite friends, neighbors and families to the performance.

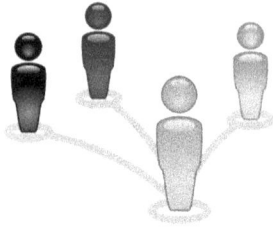

Senza Voce Video

Watch a short film or movie scene that your child hasn't seen before with the sound off.

Can he tell what was happening with Character X in the scene?
How did the character feel?
How about Character Y?
What about their faces, touches, etc., made your child feel that way?
How do the characters feel about each other?

Extra Credit: What does your child think the next interaction between the characters will be about? Does s/he think they'll feel the same way or will something change?

Fast forward and find out.

Broadway Baby

Watch a broadway show or musical theater movie with your child. Have her make up a song for one of the other characters in a scene who wasn't singing...or compose a song for "after Happily Ever After"—what happens to the main characters after the curtain goes down? (No lyrics required unless she wants to incorporate them.)

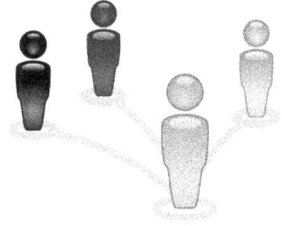

Extra Credit: Talk about why your child decided to use the tempo, dynamics, melody and harmonies that they chose.

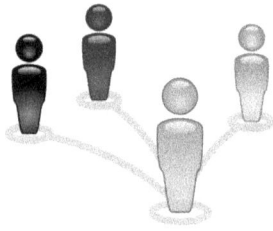

Animal Antics

Watch a short documentary or TV show about animals (Meerkat Manor or Wild Kingdom) with the sound off. After it's over, talk about what your child thought was happening during the episode and the "characters" each animal played. Replay the episode and see how close your child was to the narrator's interpretation of the scene.

Extra Credit: Talk about any similarities and differences between the interpretations and why that may be.

Touchy Touchy

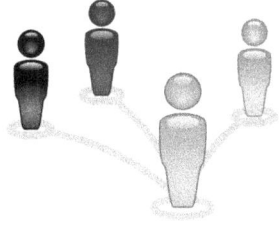

Watch a well-acted movie scene or play with lots of interaction. Write all the characters' names down one column, then make one column for touching and one column for being touched.

Have your child make a tally mark by each character's name in the appropriate column every time the character is touched or touches someone else.

At the end of the scene, tabulate the results.

Can she tell who the dominant character was just by how often they were the one doing the touching?

Try it with another TV show or movie.

Extra Credit: Visit the playground or a restaurant with your child. Do the same dominance patterns appear in the real world?

Hang with an Older Crowd

It can be downright depressing to be confined to a hospital bed or senior center. Why not use your people smarts to brighten up a hospital or senior center resident's day?

Bring along a deck of cards or a favorite board game and see if you can rustle up a game with an older crowd.

Do you enjoy reading? Read one of your favorite books to someone who's lost or is losing their eyesight.

Friends giving you fits? We'll bet those seniors have some ideas of how you could smooth things over.

Feeling directionless? Their life experiences may help you find your own path.

You're Never Too Young to Network!

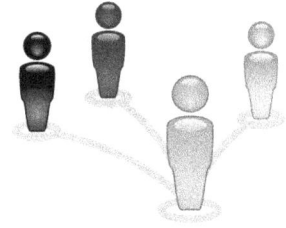

One of the most critical skills in adulthood is networking, but most adults fall into the habit of thinking that networking is just about the GET—not about the GIVE.

Who Do You Want to Meet and Why?
Draw a line down a sheet of paper and make two columns. On the left column, write your goals. On the right column, write the names of people that you could contact to help you accomplish those goals. Pin the list in a place where it's easy to edit, then add names as you come across them in conversations, articles on the computer or on television.

Reach Out
Find the person's address and write them an introductory note. Don't be shy! In this day and age, even grown-ups enjoy getting a personal letter in the mail once in awhile. Introduce yourself and share your common interest. Ask them to write back and provide either your mailing address or your parent's email address so that you can correspond.

Sharing is Caring
Do you know about an upcoming event that someone you know might be interested in attending? Tell them about it! Maybe you could go together. Did you read something about a topic that interests a friend? Send him the link, magazine or book!

Networking's not just about NEW connections
Don't forget to continue to connect with people you already know. By keeping your friends, family members and classmates up on what you're into, they may be able to provide "warm" introductions to other people that share your passions!

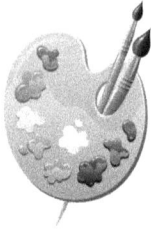

Streams, Sculptures & Screens

Introduce your kids to the visual natural masterpieces of Andy Goldsworthy. Then, go on an outdoor "explore" with your kids and your camera phone with the intention of creating your own natural mixed-medium masterpieces.

As with Andy's work, your kids can focus on whatever inspires them–stones, twigs, water, vegetables, bushes, branches, etc. "Glue" elements together with tar or sap.

The only rule is that the sculpture has to be grounded in something you found in nature in your neighborhood.

Photograph your favorites or photograph works-in-progress on your camera phone. When you get home, bring the outdoors in and upload the photos to your computer as a screen saver or desktop wallpaper. Better yet, upload them to a digital photo frame and repeat the activity as the seasons change and watch the resulting artwork shift along with the seasons.

Cardboard Kingdom

Developed by Laura Manriquez of Santa Barbara's Kids Love Art! program. Used with permission.

The parents I know always remark after birthdays and holidays that their young kids seem to have more fun with the BOXES than the toys inside. This activity makes boxes into toys with a visual/spatial project for the kids, too.

All you need is a standard-sized moving box and tempera paints, but extra construction paper, paper-towel rolls, cardboard, etc. can help make the kingdom more intricate and really flex those spatial smarts.

The resulting kingdom—or whatever your child wants the diorama to be…a firehouse…or fortress…or racetrack—is the ideal size for Polly Pocket, LEGO people, Fisher-Price little people, GI Joes or matchbox cars to call home. Which is the real genius in this project—the Kingdom can also create a home on a shelf for all the little toys you have lying around the house.

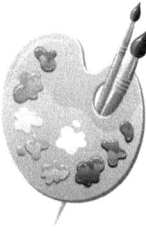

Picture Perfect Memories

Have your child sit in a comfortable, undisturbed position and breathe cyclically (in/out for the same number of beats with no breath "holds") for 2 minutes. Now, ask them to rate each image you describe from 0 (no image) to 6 (like they were actually there) for each of the following "pictures":

- Picture a blue square, green circle, and yellow triangle
- Describe your bedroom—down to the details
- Describe a pair of scissors
- Picture your mother doing a headstand
- Picture the bottom of the ocean
- Picture a photo of your favorite historical figure
- Picture how you looked at your birthday two years ago

Exercises like this one with random requests—particularly when performed during preschool and elementary school—can help your child develop their eidetic imagery capacity. Even if it doesn't help true "eidetic memory," exercises like this one can help your child better organize information for recall when necessary...in a way that's fun for kids.

Invention Breadboard

Have you ever had a great idea for
an invention or a product that makes
life easier for people? Today, get one
step closer to turning your idea into a real product with a
breadboard! Lots of people talk about product "prototypes," but
prototyping something is actually one of the last stages of the
invention process!

A breadboard can be made up of anything—it just needs
to prove that your idea could work. It doesn't need to look
anything at all like what you envision for the finished product.
There are lots of things around your house you could use to
breadboard your invention. Rolled-up magazines, straws, rope,
wire hangers, tape, glue, toilet paper rolls, old shoe boxes, old
pet leashes, etc.

Doesn't work so well on the first attempt? Keep at it!

Breadboarding gives you clues to how to make your idea work
as well as possible...and can even give you clues as to which
types of materials will work best. Let your neighbors know what
you're up to and they may have some scrap supplies they're
willing to donate to help your breadboard evolve.

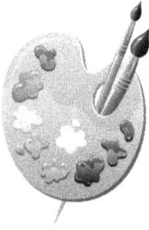

Pressed for Time

Take your child on a nature walk in your neighborhood with a grocery bag and pick up leaves and flowers that are appealing.

When you get home, open a thick book toward the back (phone books work wonders!), spread out a tissue and arrange some of your "specimens" on the tissue so that they're not touching each other.

Try different arrangements—flower petals, full flowers, twig with several leaves, leaves by themselves, etc. Cover with another tissue and flip about 100 pages, then repeat the process until all the leaves and flowers you collected have been pressed in the book. Add a few more books or a flat, heavy object on top of the original book and wait 24-48 hours. Remove the tissues, but leave the specimens in the book for a couple of weeks. Spread the options out on the table and create Nature Art with glue and paper. Let her imagination run wild with all the scenes she can create just by using the leaves and flowers she pressed.

Extra Credit: Make textured mosaics or sculptures out of other natural "specimens"—shells from the beach, pinecones, seeds, acorns, feathers, etc.

Tantalizing Tesselations

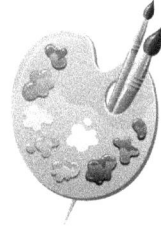

Tessellations :: A mighty big word for patterns we see all around us! From soccer balls, to tile work, to baskets, to fish scales and honeycombs.

While tessellations have always existed in nature and have been found in Moorish tilework as early as the 14th century, the person who took tessellations to a whole new level was M. C. Escher, who produced his first tessellation in 1925.

Tessellations.org defines tessellations as "repeating shapes or patterns that cover a surface without gaps or overlaps."

Flex your spatial-relations smarts and create your own tessellations with one of the following methods on tessellations. org:
• Papercut
• Tracing paper
• Line and flipping
• Gap (on the computer)

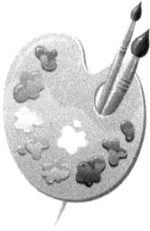

Make a Mural

Kids spend a ton of time working with 8.5 x 11" sheets of paper while sitting at a desk or table—whether you're talking worksheets, graph paper, coloring books, steno pads or binder paper. You can encourage your kids to break out of the letter-sized box with a large-scale mural that they add to all summer long. Bonus! Working with an extra-large format gives kids more practice with perspective and a chance to blend fine and gross motor prowess.

On the cheap with chalk:
Choose a sidewalk at your house, the driveway, or a public sidewalk (be sure to get appropriate neighborhood OKs!), then decide on a theme. Invite your neighbors or friends to join the fun.

Stained glass-esque:
Use a mirrored closet door or sliding glass door with dry-erase markers.

Paint a mural wall in a play room or bedroom:
The one-time drawing on the walls won't get you in trouble as a kid! Using Krylon paint, create a chalkboard wall in minutes in your house or apartment for your kids to work on during the summer.

Room Rearrangement

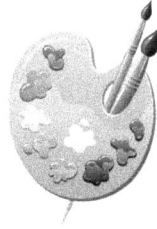

Help your child get her outside-of-school life better organized with a new bedroom arrangement!

Starting with number smarts...
First, measure the width and length of each piece of furniture, then measure the room. Decide what base number will represent a foot on a piece of graph paper. Draw the boundaries of the room on a piece of graph paper, then make note of the window placement, door placement (and radius) on the sketch.

Moving on to picture smarts...
Cut out the footprint (length and width) of each piece of furniture. Move the pieces around and test out different arrangements of the furniture on the paper.

Finally, decide on a new furniture arrangement based on your paper layouts and use your body smarts to try it out!

Will you need more storage space or a study nook? Plot out how much room she'll need for any new pieces of furniture and start a "treasure hunt" at places appropriate for her budget.

Natural States

Build on your child's blossoming naturistic and visual intelligence to connect state nature and name.

Print out (or purchase) a good sized map of the United States, then decide which of the following to "map" on top of each state:

- state flower,
- state tree,
- state bird, or
- landmark.

Print out favorite images of each and tape or glue them to the map. The natural image within the context of the shape of the state and placement on the map will help your naturalist child more easily remember which state is which (similar to the way a melody can help a child recall of the names of all fifty states).

Extra Credit: Talk about the meteorological reasons why each tree/bird/flower flourishes in each particular state. (Humid? Sunny? Warm?) Would it flourish where you live? Why or why not?

Enlightening Film Fest

Watch a movie with your child, paying close attention to set design, camera angle and lighting.

How do the changes in lighting or openness/closed feel of the set change the way your child interprets the emotional state of the actors?

Extra Credit: Are there colors or camera angles that seem to "read" as happy, sad, or scary to you?

Read a favorite book and talk about the colors, sets and camera angles your child would use to convey what's going on in each scene.

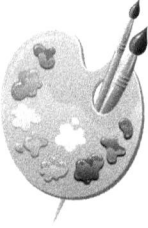

Musical Musings

Listen to a piece of music from a ballet, then have your child draw a picture or make a model of the scene they believe is occurring at that point in the ballet.

Have your child describe the picture (or model) and what about the music gave her the sense that this kind of scene was occurring.

Extra Credit: Look up what the composer intended for the piece. How closely did your child's instinct match the composer's intention?

Food with Flair

Food is ever so much more appetizing
when it's put on the plate with flair.
While traditional kids' chores generally
encompass setting the table, clearing the
table and loading the dishwasher, when
your kids help plate the food, you give them the opportunity to
put it on the plate in a way that maximizes its appeal...including
the vegetables!

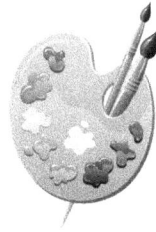

We're encouraged by nutrition experts the world over to eat a
rainbow, so get your kids into the action. Have them help you
plate dinner and, after they've designed the dishes, ask what
they think it needs. From a purely visual standpoint, more color
= more appetizing. Whether you plate the dishes individually or
present them family style, getting kids involved in this phase of
the dinnertime action may just expand their palates!

Get their creative juices flowing with some pictures of food from
colorful cookbooks or a recipe slideshow on epicurious.com.

Or, simply buy or create a face plate like this one from Fred &
Friends and just encourage your kids to give it a different look
each night:
http://www.uncommongoods.com/product/ms-food-face-plate

The Way You Make Me Feel

Play classical music pieces by different composers.

How does the music make your child feel?
What about each piece makes him/her feel that way?
Instruments used?
Chord progressions?
Tempo?
Melody?
Harmonies?

Extra Credit: Look up what the composer intended the piece to be about—or what was going on in his/her life at the time.

How closely did the reality match your child's assumptions?

Autobiographical Cube

Inspired by an activity in *Multiple Intelligences in the Elementary Classroom: A Teachers Toolkit* (Baum, Viens and Slatin. 2005)

Take a square box (or die) and put four of your child's FAVORITE multiple intelligences on the sides and two of your child's LEAST favorite intelligences.

Have your child roll the "dice." Whatever side they land on, they have to talk about one of the ways they MOST enjoy flexing that mind muscle.

Next, you roll the dice. Now talk about the way YOU most enjoy flexing that mind muscle.

Do you find similarities? Differences? Based on your child's responses, can you think of new activities or pursuits to which you'd like to introduce them?

Extra Credit: Make TWO autobiographical die. Roll them simultaneously. How does your child like to use these intelligences in concert? Some possibilities are logical and linguistic intelligence together in whodunit puzzles; creating new lyrics for music blends linguistic and musical intelligences; creating art from natural elements; etc.

Time for a Time Capsule

A "2020 Hindsight" time capsule can be a fun (and easy!) way to fill the summer with self-reflection and encourage intrapersonal growth/awareness in your children.

Wash and dry an empty plastic or glass container with a lid that can be sealed off. We recommend something quart-sized. Label the jar "2020 Hindsight" with a Sharpie. Then, have your child add things to the jar that will give their future self a glimpse into what s/he was like now. Some ideas of what to put into the jar:

- picture of the type of job she would like to have as an adult;
- a favorite toy;
- photos of best friends with their names on the back of each photo;
- the DVD jacket picture of a favorite movie;
- a CD of his favorite songs (with names and artists written on it);
- a list of current favorite books to read;
- wrapper or her favorite food(s);
- a photo/brochure from the place he would most like to visit in the future;
- a baggie of how much allowance she earns each week;
- a note about who he imagines he will be when he opens the time capsule.

Decide on a place to stash it where it will stay undisturbed until you open it.

Wordless Walk

Make a date to go for a wordless walk with your child each evening.

Use the opportunity to silently reflect on your days, just enjoying the sounds of nature as you stroll away the day's stresses. Think about what you both enjoyed most about your days and what you want to change tomorrow.

When you get back to the house, you can either talk about the day's ups and downs for you both or draw or journal about them.

Just Dreamy

No matter whether you believe that dreams can help you solve problems, give insights into what's to come into your life, or are simply strange jumbles of emotions and images from your day... they do offer an interesting look at your unconscious and can be great fodder for analysis or creative writing.

We all dream every night...about once every 90 minutes or so. And even if you're lucky enough to remember your dreams immediately upon waking, most times the details quickly fade and don't get stored in an accessible memory bank. Instead of having your child attempt to wake up enough to write down their dreams first thing in the morning or by the light of the moon, give them a voice recorder to save their recollections immediately upon waking.

Just getting kids in the habit of recording the way their brain processes information while asleep can improve their intrapersonal awareness. Plus, there's no more fun breakfast conversation than the crazy dreams each family member had the night before.

When you tuck your kids in at night, talk to them about things they might want to record when they wake up:
• key points of the plot
• any dialogue from the dream
• who was in it?
• any moods/feelings
• where did it take place?
• did anything stand out as strange?

Weather Wordle

If you haven't already discovered Wordle.com, this activity will give you a fun introduction to this creative tool as well as a creative way to get your kids talking about all the natural phenomena that affect people every day around the world.

Come up with a list of all the natural phenomena you can think of...both pleasant and more concerning, and how thinking about those occurrences make you feel.

Input the list of phenomena into Wordle and then choose color, font and text direction to mash them all up in a Wordle.

Annual Autobiography

The important people, places and events that made the past year memorable are more easily recollected right now than they ever will be again.

Today, make sure you never forget what made you grow and change this past year with your own yearbook.

Be sure to add captions that will jog your memory about each picture when you want to walk down memory lane 80 years from now. You might want to even include longer passages or journal entries about events you don't necessarily have pictures of. Let your memories put you back in the action, and describe as vividly as you can what you felt, along with the sounds, the sights, the smells, etc.

A great online tool to publish your own yearbook is blurb.com.

Start a Bucket List

Have everyone in your family make a list of 20 things they'd like to see/experience during their lifetimes. Compare notes and make plans to accomplish at least one goal per person within the next six months.

Extra Credit: Did any family members have any similar goals? Did any of the goals surprise you? What do your goals say about each person's individual personality?

Celebrating Citizenship

No matter what country you live in, people the world over have their own traditions for celebrating citizenship. Play some national anthems with your child and read the English versions of the lyrics together.

English versions of anthem lyrics for a vast array of countries can be found here:
http://www.lyricsondemand.com/miscellaneouslyrics/nationalanthemslyrics/u.html

The U.S. Navy Band has streaming MP3s of national anthems for many countries here:
http://www.navyband.navy.mil/Anthems/national_anthems.htm

Talk together about the kinds of instruments you hear in the anthems and how the music makes your child feel. Then, talk about the similar words that are found in each piece you listen to.

If your child was to create an anthem for a group—family, school, church, scouts, country—what instruments would he choose to incorporate? What words would he use in the anthem to tell others how it feels to be a part of that group?

Alien Invasion

*Adapted from a Chicago City Parks &
Rec activity recommendation. Used with
permission.*

See a familiar outdoor setting with new
eyes as you and your child pretend to be aliens on a mission to
explore our planet and report back to your leader. Feel free to
dress up or define your own rules for how you
- sense things (do you see with your hands? smell with your
  feet?);
- move (do you fly? hop? walk on hands AND legs?); or
- speak (do they speak pig latin or another made-up language
  on your planet? or just English?).

Start out discovering new things together and dreaming up new
perspectives. Is a tree an earthling? Is a shell a telephone? Then
split up and explore the space before reuniting a few minutes
later to talk about everything you discovered on your mission.

If your child really enjoys this activity, try it again in other
environments like the grocery store or around the house.

Innerspace List Poems

Adapted with permission from the Chicago City Park District's "Once Upon a Day Camp" Guide

Using a piece of butcher paper, draw an outline of your child's body with a magic marker or crayon. Ask your child to think about what they think is happening to them on the inside. If your child doesn't understand, give them examples like "my heart beats like the hoofs of a running horse" or "after recess, my legs feel wiggly like jello".

Now that she has the idea, give her 15 minutes to fill the outline with pictures of the wonderful world that's living inside of her. (If she is very young, have your child tell you what she envisions and you can draw symbols and pictures for her.)

Tell your child that a list poem is a poem with a new idea on each line. Then, ask her to make up a list poem about the pictures they just drew.

Extra Credit: Listen first to the biographical introduction to each poet and then as the poets themselves read their poems in *Poetry Speaks Expanded: Hear Poets Read Their Own Work From Tennyson to Plath* (Elise Paschen, 2007). Then talk about what each poet must have been feeling/experiencing when each poem was written. What does your child think each poet's personality was like? What makes your child think so?

Self Smart Activity

All of us have hot buttons that cause us to react in not so great ways. Today, brainstorm some of the types of situations or comments that really push your buttons, then brainstorm some ways to diffuse the situation and try acting them out at home.

A few tactics to try:
• add humor,
• look at the situation from the other person's point of view,
• excuse yourself for a few moments or minutes to collect your thoughts,
• redirect the conversation to another topic,
• find a way to compromise.

By practicing better reactions, you'll be less likely to melt down in the heat of the moment.

Be Virtuous

We think most parents will agree that the greatest gift we can give our children is the authentic self-esteem that comes from developing their virtues.

The Virtues Project helps parents to awaken the qualities of character that exist in their kids' potential. Help your kids understand what it means to become compassionate, courageous, respectful, confident or purposeful by doing daily or weekly Family Virtues Picks here:
http://www.virtuesproject.com/family.html

Each pick reveals a different virtue, what it means, and how to become more successful at each virtue.

Limerick Epitaphs

Talk to your child about what an epitaph is (a brief poem or other writing in praise of a someone who has passed away so that others could get a sense of who the person was).

Then read some limericks to/with your child so that they understand the structure of this type of poem. (First, second and fifth lines rhyme with 9 syllables each; the third and fourth lines rhyme with 5 syllables each.)

Have your child dream up some limericks that they would use to describe the lives of people they know or favorite characters in books, so that people who don't know them might have a better idea of who each person once was.

Extra Credit: Read selections from a book like *Fire in the Sea: An Anthology of Poetry and Art* (Sue Cowing, 1996) and compare what each of the authors was writing about with what life must have been like for them in their respective corners of the world.

Starstruck Storytime

There's no better time than warm, summertime nights to stargaze.
Connecting the dots in the sky with the mythology from different cultures can leave your linguistic child starstruck. Check books out of the library telling the stories of each constellation.

A couple of titles to consider or seek out:

Star Lore of All Ages (Olcott, 1996).
A collection of myths, legends and facts about the constellations in the Northern Hemisphere.

New Patterns in the Sky (Staal, 1996).
Myths and legends about the stars.

Extra Credit: What patterns do you and your child see in the stars? Do you see any different animals, objects or people?
Have your child make up an original myth at bedtime about the different patterns you saw together.

Poetry Puzzle

Check out a poetry anthology from the library that covers the work of poets from several decades or centuries and compare the word choices of the authors from different eras.

How has the English language changed over time? What words don't you hear anymore? What new words does your child love in each poem?

Extra Credit: Grab magazines, junk mail, newspapers, etc. from around the house. Give your child 5 minutes to tear or cut out words that they like or that grab their attention.

Then, have your child use as many of those words as possible to create a "when" poem.

Basic structure:
When I _fill in the blank_ (role or experience)
I _fill in the blank_ (action)
like a _fill in the blank_ (noun)
I _fill in the blank_ (action)
and _fill in the blank_ (action)
When I _fill in the blank_ (repeat role or experience)

Length doesn't matter, nor does rhyming.

Scripted Storytime

If your child cringes at the thought of reading traditional books, but loves movies, try having him read screenplays with you from some movie favorites, available on IMSDB.com.

(Or, if your child is still an early or pre-reader, read a few scenes from the script to him.)

Whenever he doesn't know a word, look it up on dictionary. com or thesaurus.com. After reading a few scenes from the screenplay, have him tell you his five favorite new words from the script. For the rest of the day, try to use the new vocabulary words in conversation.

Journal Jar

Journals have the unique ability to not only develop writing chops, but also help kids get a handle on their emotions, moods and reactions on a journey of self-discovery and reflection.

But just getting your child a diary and encouraging him to write in it daily may not be enough to get the pencil moving on the page.

Brainstorm topics with your child that he would enjoy exploring either that week, that month or over the year, and put them on individual scraps of paper in a journal jar. Google "journal prompts" if you and your child are having trouble coming up with ideas.

Then, have your child pick one prompt out of the journal jar each day and spend 10-20 minutes writing about the topic.

Worldly Words

Learn about a different aspect of the world around you each week! Brainstorm topics about the natural world that your child finds interesting, then put those topics in a hat or bowl. Have your child draw one topic each week to learn about together.

As you read each week, highlight the different informational text features that help aid learning. For instance, bolded or italicized type, tables of contents, labeled drawings, captioned boxes, diagrams/charts and using vocabulary context to help decipher the meaning of challenging words.

Use a variety of informational media (web sites, news articles, magazines, books) to illustrate how learning strategies shift by media type. Then, build on these early strategies and teach your child to skim, scan, and summarize. First skim the text— ask your child questions like, what do you notice on the page or think the key points might be? Then, scan it and digest the information slowly. Finally, talk to each other about what you just read. What was important? What was most interesting about the book or article? What does your child want to find out more about as a result of reading the book or article?

You may find yourself throwing out the hat topics and delving deeper into unexpected arenas!

Color Decoding

Depending on your child's reading level, use color coding to help kids see patterns in spelling, vocabulary or grammar.

For instance, if your child is learning to read, find an article in a magazine at home or print out a story on the computer that your child wants to read.

Read the piece together and have your child highlight long vowels and short ones, then look at the piece as a whole and see what patterns they can find. For example, a silent e makes a vowel long, if you see "ght" at the end of the word, the "i" is long, if you only see one vowel in the word and it's at the end, the vowel is long.

If your child is older, color-code word prefixes, roots and suffixes. Can she predict the meaning of each prefix/root/suffix based on the meaning of the whole word? See how close she came on prefixsuffix.com.

If your child is learning sentence structure, use the different highlighters to diagram parts of each sentence and illustrate the 10 basic sentence patterns found in English on: http://www.towson.edu/ows/SentPatt.htm

Shape Poetry

A shape poem is one that describes an object and is written in the shape of the object. To get your child's creative juices flowing, Google examples of shape poetry online.

Next, have your child pick an object to write about. Brainstorm words that you both think of when you see the shape or would use to describe the object.

If your child is under 7 years old, have him first draw the picture, then give you the words he would use to describe it as you fill in the shape with his description. If your child is over 7, ask her to write the poem in the object's shape. Encourage your child to use different colors to further embellish their work.

Extra Credit: Try making a picture with multiple objects, each filled in with a shape poem. (sun, rainbow, cloud, tree, grass and flower; a farm with multiple animals.)

Family-nyms

These days, it seems like everyone is LOLing about something every time they TTY. "Net Lingo" has everyone from kindergarteners to senior citizens speaking or typing in acronyms lately.

Using acronyms can also give your family a secret language of your own either around the house or out in public without letting guests or passers-by in on your secrets.

Some ideas to get you rolling:
- EOT (elbows off the table), at restaurants
- SEH (send 'em home), when you're ready for a play date to come to a close
- GTGPP! (got to go to the bathroom) Keep your eyes peeled for a public restroom!

Want more acronym fun? Play Acronymble! You can DIY or buy the real thing.

Here's how to play:
Have each family member pick a letter randomly or pick Scrabble tiles/magnetic letters out of a bag. Players need to decide what the letters in the acronym stand for out of the letters that are picked. For example, if you received the letters E.K.M.F., you might write, "Everyday Kids Make Faces." Each player then votes for his favorite acronym—but you can't vote for your own!

The beauty of this game is that there are no right and wrong answers...and it's different every time.

Magnetic Moments

Magnetic poetry can be a fun way for your kids to practice reading, vocabulary, sentence or poetry structure, and generally get creative. There's no need to feel limited by what's available for purchase right out of the box, though! Thanks to printable magnetic sheets for inkjet printers, you can DIY and create magnetic poetry kits that are perfect for both your child's reading level and interests! You can typically purchase these sheets at your neighborhood office store (Staples, Office Depot, etc.) or you can buy them online here.

Recommended sight words to include based on reading level for grades K-3:
http://www.kidzone.ws/dolch/index.htm

Recommended vocabulary words (based on what's likely to be found on standardized tests) for grades 2-8:
http://flocabulary.s3.amazonaws.com/pdfs/flat/word-up-word-lists.pdf

Have your child help you decide which additional nouns, verbs and adjectives to include so that his poetry feels personal.

You'll Hit It Out of the Park with Me In Your Corner

One of the most critical vocabulary elements to nail down when learning American English (or any culture's language) is the use of idioms.

An idiom, as defined by dictionary.com, is a group of words whose meaning cannot be predicted from the meanings of the constituent words. For example, "It was raining cats and dogs."

Being able to understand and use idioms successfully also makes the art of language more playful...and fun for kids. Key into one of your child's favorite pastimes and look at the idioms that have one meaning in the pastime...and a different one entirely in every day language.

Have a field day with these sports idioms:
englishclub.com/vocabulary/idioms-sports.htm

See which music idioms ring a bell here:
englishclub.com/ref/Idioms/Music/index.htm

Shed light on these nature idioms:
usingenglish.com/reference/idioms/cat/27.html

Or try to bat a thousand with math idioms:
idiomconnection.com/number.html

Get Good Stories Rolling

According to the Common Core writing standards, "each year in their writing, students should demonstrate increasing sophistication in all aspects of language use, from vocabulary and syntax to the development and organization of ideas, and they should address increasingly demanding content and sources."

One fun way to practice and hone writing skills is through storytelling. We all know how important story arcs are in order to keep readers engaged in fiction...but similar arcs are equally important in essays and informational texts. Rory's Story Cubes can help your kids come up with story ideas and flex their word smarts in ten million ways for less than $10. (Literally!)

You can also DIY with a few verbs and nouns in ziploc bags. Maybe even use some of the words your child selected in our magnetic poetry activity!

Reading Recall

Whether you're reading during the school year or logging your minutes reading with Scholastic's Summer Reading Challenge over the summer, we're sure your young learners are making lots of visits to their school libraries, local libraries or bookstores.

But what good is all that reading if you don't remember what you read? Make your reading lists a family affair (meaning ALL of you read the books--either together or separately), then challenge each other to a game of Reading Recall!

Create the Game:
Grab some index cards and a pen. Write a character AND book name on one index card. Use a second index card to write something about who the character was or what happened to him/her in the book. Create these "pairs" for all of the books you read during the week.

Game Play:
Just like the traditional game of Memory, shuffle the cards and place all of them face down. Turning over 2 cards per turn, see who can correctly match and collect the most pairs during the game. Up the ante each week by adding additional book pairs to the mix.

www.ingramcontent.com/pod-product-compliance
Lightning Source LLC
Chambersburg PA
CBHW060950040426
42445CB00011B/1090